F
T
THE CHURCH

Mary's Message
*with* Prayers *and*
Devotions

Timothy Tindal-Robertson
and Donal Anthony Foley

*All booklets are published
thanks to the generosity of the supporters
of the Catholic Truth Society*

# Contents

All rights reserved. First published 2021
by The Incorporated Catholic Truth Society.
42-46 Harleyford, Road, London SE11 5AY.
Tel: 020 7640 0042. www.ctsbooks.org.
© 2021 Timothy Tindal-Robertson and
Donal Anthony Foley.

ISBN 978 1 78469 656 6

# Fatima's Message to the Church Today

The first edition of this booklet was published in 2016, some six months before the announcement of a marvellous and quite unexpected development that caused the celebration on 13th May 2017 of the one hundredth anniversary of Our Lady's first apparition at Fatima to become a truly unique event. For only a few weeks beforehand, on 23rd March 2017, it was announced by the Vatican that on that day Pope Francis had approved the second miracle that was required for the canonisation of Blessed Francisco and Jacinta Marto. It was further announced that the date and place for the ceremony of canonisation would not be decided until the next consistory to be held in Rome, on 20th April, less than one month before the anniversary on 13th May. It was at that consistory that Pope Francis announced he would canonise Francisco and Jacinta just over three weeks later in the Portuguese shrine, on 13th May 2017, in the course of an apostolic visit to Fatima on 12-13th May to commemorate the centenary of Our Lady's apparitions.

"There are no mere coincidences in the plans of divine Providence", Pope St John Paul II famously observed, in referring to the assassination attempt on his life on 13th May 1981. The miracle required for the canonisation of the two seers was a further sign that this development was more than a mere coincidence, for it concerned the miraculous and permanent healing of a five year old boy, whose skull was fractured and brain tissue lost, when he fell on to a pavement from a third floor balcony.

The parents were told that the boy's chances of surviving were low, and if he did survive, his recovery would be very slow, and leave him with severe cognitive disabilities or even remaining in a semi-comatose state. When his condition worsened the parents appealed to a Carmelite convent for prayers. It so happened that there were relics of Blessed Francisco and Jacinta on the altar next to the tabernacle, and one of the nuns was inspired to pray, "Shepherds, save this child, who is a child like you". The community, the parents and many others joined in making this appeal to God for a cure, through the intercession of the two seers. Within one week, the child was discharged from the hospital, and his father recounted at the press conference in Fatima how since then the boy has been completely well, with no symptoms or after effects: "he has the same intelligence as before the accident, the same character, everything is the same". In medical terms, his cure was inexplicable.

## More than a 'Mere Coincidence'

In this miracle, a brain-damaged child is restored to normal health through the intercession of the first child saints in the history of the Church to die not as martyrs, but in the ordinary course of their family life. It is significant that Our Lady chose three uneducated children from a very simple village background, the youngest offspring of two devout and large Catholic families, to receive her message for the salvation of sinners (*Mk* 2:17), and the deliverance of the Church from contemporary evils caused by the denial and rejection of God that has spread throughout the world in multiple forms in our time. Is not their canonisation on the one hundredth anniversary of Our Lady's apparition, more than a 'mere coincidence' that divine Providence has given to us, in order to highlight the importance of Our Lady's message in the life of the family, which is "as it were, a church in the home" (*Lumen Gentium* [*LG*] 11), the domestic Church, as lived according to the heroic example of Saints Francisco and Jacinta? And is this not even more true when one considers that this development has come at a time when the Christian family today is facing unprecedented threats from a secularised society, which has divorced itself from Christian morality, accepts adultery, co-habitation and alternative forms of marriage, advocates abortion as a right on a huge scale, and even believes in manipulating one's own human nature, as given to each individual by God?

These damaging trends in society have inevitably impacted the Church, which as a result has suffered a very serious decline in vocations, and also in the numbers of Catholics who continue to practice their faith. This process has been documented by Professor Stephen Bullivant of St Mary's Catholic University, Twickenham, in a detailed academic study full of statistics and tables, *Mass Exodus: Catholic Disaffiliation in Britain and America since Vatican II*, published by Oxford University Press in 2019.

## Our Lady's Requests

A century ago Our Lady of Fatima gave us a specific warning, in her prophecy on 13th July 1917, that such developments would arise if people did not cease offending God, when she spoke of the "errors of Russia", meaning the denial and rejection of God. In our time it is this spirit of the denial and rejection of God which has come to dominate the culture of present-day society, in the form of secularism, relativism, and living one's life as if God does not exist, thereby ignoring and rejecting the teaching of the Gospel and the Church, which has been marginalised, or treated as irrelevant. In order to prevent such a scenario from arising, all that Our Lady asked people to do, was to fulfil her requests for prayer, penance in reparation for sin which offends God, sacrifices for the conversion of sinners – the primary purpose of Jesus's incarnation – and especially to make the Five First Saturdays devotion

of reparation to her Immaculate Heart, and to pray the Rosary every day. These requests were so simple that very young uneducated shepherd children, no older than seven, nine and ten, were able to fulfil them to a heroic degree, as Pope St John Paul II stated at their beatification on 13th May 2000. Thereby Francisco and Jacinta were raised up to become saints, and in due course were canonised by Pope Francis on 13th May 2017.

With the exception of a few countries – and some significant examples in the past century of how compliance with her requests, especially the recitation of the Rosary when taken up by large numbers, has delivered the Church from grave evils and restored its position in society – it would appear that, despite the unprecedented approval for Our Lady's message, in the teaching and acts of five popes, these requests from Mary most holy, Mother of God and of the Church, have for no apparent reason been disregarded by the great majority of bishops, as well as priests and the laity, particularly in Western Europe.

While it is true that Fatima is a private revelation and voluntary devotion which one is not obliged to accept, nevertheless, since Our Lady's message has received such unanimous papal approval, it is difficult to understand why so many Church leaders throughout the world have not followed the example and teaching of the popes who, from the reign of Pius XII onwards, have strongly urged acceptance of Our Lady's message, none more so than Pope Francis, as we will see.

## The Devotion of the Popes

Pope St Paul VI was the first pope to visit Fatima, on 13th May 1967, and meet Sr Lucia, who he presented to the huge crowd outside the basilica, thereby signifying his approval of the message which it was her mission to proclaim in the Church. While there, he blessed statues of Our Lady of Fatima, one of which was presented to the World Apostolate of Fatima in England. Then in May 1982 Pope St John Paul II went to Fatima for the first time, to thank Our Lady for saving his life from the assassination attempt in the previous year, and his homily on 13th May was the first time a pope had given formal teaching on Our Lady's message. The Church had accepted the message of Fatima, said the Pope, because its basic content is the same as the first words the Messiah addressed to humanity: "Repent and believe in the gospel" (*Mk* 1:15); and later, in a message to the Bishop of Fatima dated 1st October 1997, the Pope said that Fatima was certainly one of the greatest signs of the times "because its message announces many of the later events and conditions them on the response to its appeals" (*Message of Fatima*, pp. 76, 77).

## Our Lady and the Rosary

The truth of this statement has tragically been borne out by the unceasing wars and ever-increasing persecution of the Church in countries throughout the world, and this situation continues principally because sadly so many in the Church have not yet understood the need to comply with Our Lady's requests. Pope St John Paul II fulfilled Our Lady's request for the consecration of Russia by his act of 25th March 1984, but the counterpart of that request, the Five First Saturdays devotion, which pertains to the Church, has only been fulfilled in a small number of parishes and dioceses. Equally important, as pertaining to individuals to fulfil in their daily life, is Our Lady's request in each of her six apparitions, to pray the Rosary every day for peace. In her final apparition on 13th October, she revealed, "I am the Lady of the Rosary", and in the Litany of Loreto she is addressed as Queen of the most Holy Rosary and Queen of Peace. If we are serious about obtaining peace, we should take equally seriously Our Lady's request for daily recitation of the Rosary. The history of the Rosary's remarkable power to overcome evil, convert people, bring peace in society and raise up saints, is admirably documented in *Champions of the Rosary* by Fr Donald Calloway, MIC.

In a video message to the people of Portugal at the time of his visit to Fatima in May 2017, Pope Francis urged them: "Never abandon the Rosary. Never abandon the Rosary. Pray the Rosary, as she asked". After the stupendous miracle of the sun on 13th October 1917, that was seen by around seventy thousand people who had made the pilgrimage to Fatima from all over Portugal, many on foot, there was no longer any doubt that Our Lady had been appearing to the three child seers, and a nation-wide movement of people praying the Rosary every day sprang up spontaneously. The result, in the course of the next two decades, was the miraculous and peaceful transformation of Portugal, as Cardinal Cerejeira, Patriarch of Lisbon, testified. The republican party, which had fiercely repressed and persecuted the Church after it overthrew the monarchy in 1908, and had even publicly vowed to eliminate it, gradually subsided and died out, while the Church emerged stronger than ever, with numerous conversions and vocations.

## The exceptional role of the Mother of God

In the light of similar historical examples, and the teaching on the Rosary of Popes Leo XIII and St John Paul II, as well as great Marian saints such as Louis de Montfort, author of *The Secret of the Rosary*, there is every reason to believe that a similar transformation could take place in our country. All that is required is for bishops and priests to work with the laity in order to build up a national movement of people praying the Rosary every day. The great virtue of the Rosary, in the words of Pope St John Paul II, in his Apostolic Letter *Rosarium Virginis Mariae*, is that it puts one "in living communion with the mysteries of Christ", whenever and wherever it is prayed with devotion. The Rosary is an ideal method of praying because it is simple, young children can easily become proficient in it, and it can be prayed anywhere at any time throughout the week, especially when many people in work are unable to get to daily Mass. Many popes and Marian saints have demonstrated the great spiritual benefits that the Rosary can bring to the lives of the faithful, through assisting them on the path to personal sanctification. There is no doubt that such a movement at a national level would make an important contribution to the urgent task of re-evangelisation; and history has demonstrated the power of the Rosary to counter difficulties that today confront families, in terms of the pressure to conform to purely secular values that undermine the Faith, and that the government is seeking to enforce in schools.

In the eighth chapter of *Lumen Gentium*, there is an admirable account of the exceptional role of "the Mother of God in the Mystery of Christ and the Church", as it is entitled. In heaven, "she persists, with many pleas, in winning the gifts of divine salvation for her Son's brethren… still involved in dangers and difficulties. For this reason the Blessed Virgin is called upon in the Church under the titles of Advocate, Auxiliatrix, Adjutrix, Mediatrix" (op. cit., n. 62). This is why we need to turn to her for help in overcoming the trials we face today.

### England's Devotion to Our Lady

As we saw with the amazing response to the re-dedication of England as Mary's Dowry, on Sunday 29th March 2020, and last year in the great response to the Rosary at the Coast initiative, many of the faithful have a deep love for the Blessed Virgin, and would welcome and support initiatives to foster her devotions. There was a similar response when the World Apostolate of Fatima in England and Wales, brought the national Pilgrim Virgin statue, presented to England by Pope Paul VI in 1967, to be crowned by Cardinal Nichols in Westminster Cathedral, at a special Mass in her honour in February 2017.

(see: *https://worldfatima-englandwales.org.uk/national-pilgrim-virgin-statue-of-our-lady-of-fatima/*)

So many people packed in to the cathedral, the doors had to be closed to prevent overcrowding, thousands of petitions were accepted and forwarded to her shrine in Fatima, to be placed under her statue, and many people presented Our Lady with voluntary offerings of personal items of gold and silver jewellery, in thanksgiving for her visitation and as a contribution to the cost of the silver-gilt crown, that had been specially created in Lisbon for the visitations of her statue to the cathedrals of England and Wales, which took place throughout the Centenary Year of 2017.

## A Mother who Desires Everyone's Salvation

Referring to the global spirit of the denial and rejection of God, in his homily at Fatima Pope St John Paul II said that the Mother, who desires everyone's salvation, intervened because she cannot "keep silence on what undermines the very basis of their salvation", and that her care extends to the whole of humanity, "menaced by apostasy and threatened by moral degradation". Is that not the situation in which we find ourselves today? He then explained that Fatima proposes the consecration to the Immaculate Heart of Mary, because that means "consecrating this world to the pierced Heart of the Saviour, bringing it back to the very source of its redemption"; and that Mary's appeal "must be taken up by generation after generation, in accordance with the ever new 'signs of the time'".

Pope St John Paul II's act of 25th March 1984, which fulfilled Our Lady's request for the consecration of Russia, brought about the peaceful collapse of the Soviet Union, one of the world's greatest military superpowers, which is documented in my book, *Fatima, Russia & Pope John Paul II*. As a result the countries of Eastern Europe that had been overrun by the Soviet Union after World War II, were delivered from the atheist persecution that had caused untold suffering to millions of people, and were free to join the European Union. This prodigious miracle, which astonishingly has hardly been recognised, is a shining example of the power of Our Lady's intercession with God, and hence an indication of what can be expected when the Church complies with her requests.

Thus by his teaching and his acts with regard to Fatima, Pope St John Paul II has provided the Church with every reason and incentive to follow his example so as to bring about its re-evangelisation and resurrection, which is so greatly needed at this time. Accordingly, for the sake of our children and grandchildren, who are so vulnerable to the adverse influences threatening the Church and the Christian family, may we respectfully petition our bishops to respond to the heartfelt prayer of the faithful, to actively promote the message of Fatima, in particular the Five First Saturdays devotion and praying the Rosary every day. (see: *https://worldfatima-englandwales.org.uk/the-five-first-saturdays-devotion-explained/*)

In his final act, Pope St John Paul II entrusted the whole of the third millennium to the intercession of the Immaculate Heart of Mary, at the Jubilee Mass of the Bishops in St Peter's on Sunday 8th October 2000. This was the largest gathering of bishops at St Peter's since Vatican II.

### Consecrated Priests

When he went on pilgrimage to Fatima in May 2010, Pope Benedict XVI consecrated all the world's priests to the Immaculate Heart of Mary, and warned that in our time "the Faith in many places seems like a light in danger of being snuffed out for ever". He also said that "we would be mistaken to think that Fatima's prophetic mission is complete" and that he looked forward to "the fulfilment of the prophecy of the triumph of the Immaculate Heart of Mary" (*Shepherds of Fatima,* pp. 34, 41).

It is clear that both these popes strongly approved the message of Fatima, and how closely it relates to the destiny of the Church and the world in our time. Following their legacy, Pope Francis strongly endorsed the importance of Our Lady's message for the Church, in a number of pronouncements on the occasion of his visit to the shrine, on 12-13th May 2017, for the canonisation of Francisco and Jacinta.

At his General Audience on Wednesday 10th May 2017, the Pope said that he was going to Fatima "to entrust to the Virgin the temporal and eternal destinies of humanity". When he came to the site of the apparitions, the Pope said he intended to present Mary with a "bouquet of the most beautiful 'flowers' that Jesus entrusted to my care: that is, my brothers and sisters from all over the world who were redeemed by his blood." Then the Pope said: "I will give you all to Our Lady, asking her to whisper to each one of you: 'My Immaculate Heart will be your refuge and the way that will lead you to God'" using the very words that Our Lady spoke to Lucia on 13th June 1917. He went on to say: "if we want to be Christian, we must be Marian; in a word, we have to acknowledge the essential, vital and providential relationship uniting Our Lady to Jesus, a relationship that opens before us the way leading to him".

With the canonisation of Francisco and Jacinta, said Pope Francis, "I want to propose to the whole Church to have the heart of children", in a reference to the admonition of Jesus: "unless you turn and become like children, you will never enter the kingdom of heaven. Whoever humbles himself like this child, he is the greatest in the kingdom of heaven. Whoever receives one such child in my name receives me" (*Mt* 18:3-5). It is also a clear reference to the fact that the three seers chosen by Our Lady were children.

### The Divine Mercy and Fatima

These pronouncements by Pope Francis are effectively summed up in his powerful endorsement of the two great messages of the Divine Mercy and Fatima, which he said had been strongly promoted by Pope St John Paul II:

"Let us accept these messages so that they fill our hearts".

This statement is singularly appropriate, since the heart is the key to understanding the deep spiritual significance of Fatima, at the level of the individual and at the level of the Church. For it is a message with an appeal to our hearts from the Immaculate Heart of the holy Mother of God, overflowing with the merciful love of Jesus for the souls of sinners and those, so numerous today, who are indifferent to or reject God. Captivated by the beautiful Lady from heaven, and the prospect of going there, the three seers, with the charming openness of children, responded with all their hearts to her requests, and accordingly were raised up to become saints – the vocation which God desires for everyone (cf. *LG* 39, citing *Ep* 5:25-26).

In his homily at the beatification of Francisco and Jacinta on 13th May 2000, Pope St John Paul II said that Francisco "attained a true form of mystical union with the Lord", and he compared Jacinta with St Paul writing to the Colossians (1:24), regarding her extraordinary acceptance of suffering "for the sake of Christ's body, the Church". On the following webpage is a selection of sayings of the two child saints which illustrate their remarkable experiences and spirituality: *https://worldfatima-englandwales.org.uk/wp-content/uploads/2018/01/sayingsfandj.pdf.*

Through the inspiring story of how the lives of the seers changed after meeting the Angel in 1916, and then even more after their exchanges with Our Lady in 1917, there is traced out an assured path to heaven through life's trials and challenges, that can easily be followed by all under the consoling maternal guidance of Our Lady of Fatima.

After the first apparition on 13th May in 1917, little Jacinta kept on exclaiming enthusiastically, "Oh, what a beautiful Lady", and that night broke her word to keep quiet by telling her parents everything they had seen and heard. "There was something within me that wouldn't let me keep quiet", she tearfully told Francisco and Lucia. That was how the apparition became known, and immediately brought down upon them the suffering which Our Lady had foretold, as the children experienced the doubt, disbelief and opposition of their own parents.

The same effect has been produced throughout salvation history, whenever someone has experienced a true, interior and heartfelt personal encounter with the living God. This is what caused the hearts of Jesus's disciples – and countless others in the ensuing centuries – to "burn within them" (cf. *Lk* 24:32). The divine experience planted in them such unquenchable joy and conviction that it "wouldn't let them keep quiet", and thereafter for the sake of proclaiming the gospel they were willing to "bear all the sufferings he wills to send you, as an act of reparation for the conversion of sinners" (cf. *Col* 1:24; *2 Tm* 2:12). It was on these terms that Our Lady asked the children, "are you willing to offer yourselves to God?" and when they responded, "Yes," she told them they would have much to suffer, "but the grace of God will be your comfort".

## Taking up One's Cross

Conversion, says the *Catechism of the Catholic Church*, is accomplished in daily life by, among other things, accepting suffering and enduring persecution. "Taking up one's cross each day and following Jesus is the surest way of penance" (*CCC* 1435, citing *Lk* 9:23). The lives of Saints Francisco and Jacinta show that the message of Fatima is the extension to the Church of this gospel-witnessing experience, in a manner adapted to the circumstances of our times through the mediation of Our Lady and her Immaculate Heart, in order to participate in Jesus's mission to save souls: "I came not to call the righteous but sinners" (*Mk* 2:17). In his General Audience on 17th May 2000, after beatifying Francisco and Jacinta, Pope St John Paul II described the message of Fatima as "a message of conversion and hope… which is the true Gospel of Christ."

Angels "belong to him [Christ]…and are messengers of his saving plan", we are informed by the *Catechism of the Catholic Church* (*CCC* 331). In 1916 an angel appeared to the children and told them that the Hearts of Jesus and Mary had "designs of mercy" upon them, namely, to offer up sacrifices in reparation for sins and the conversion of sinners. "Conversion", wrote Pope St John Paul II, "is the most concrete expression of the working of love and of the presence of mercy in the human world" (*Dives in Misericordia*, 6). God's infinite grace and mercy for sinners out of his desire for their conversion and salvation, mediated through the Immaculate Heart of Mary, is the thread running through the apparitions at Fatima.

The Pardon Prayer which the Angel taught the seers in his first apparition comprises the virtues of faith, hope and charity which "are the pledge of the presence and action of the Holy Spirit in the faculties of the human being" (Q 384: *Compendium of the Catechism of the Catholic Church*). The seers repeated this grace-filled prayer for hours on end, and this prepared them for the apparitions of Our Lady in the following year.

## The Grace of God

In her first apparition, after Our Lady had told them that the grace of God would comfort them in their suffering, she opened her hands for the first time, and communicated "a light so intense that as it streamed from her hands, its rays penetrated our hearts and the innermost depths of our souls, making us see ourselves in God who was that light, more clearly than we see ourselves in the best of mirrors. Then, moved by an interior impulse that was also communicated to us, we fell on our knees, repeating in our hearts:

'O most holy Trinity, I adore you! My God, my God, I love you in the most Blessed Sacrament'" (*Fatima in Lucia's own Words* [*FILOW*], pp. 175, 176).

Afterwards Francisco said, "I loved seeing the Angel, but I loved still more seeing Our Lady. What I loved most of all was to see Our Lord in that light from Our Lady which penetrated our hearts. I love God so much. But he is very sad because of so many sins."

This profound mystical experience through Our Lady kindled in their hearts that fire of the love of God which did not burn them, so that they were willing to accept whatever suffering he would send for the conversion and salvation of sinners. In the words of Pope Benedict XVI, the Lady "from heaven" was "the Teacher who introduced the little seers to a deep knowledge of the love of the Blessed Trinity and led them to savour God himself as the most beautiful reality of human existence" (*Shepherds of Fatima*, p. 38). Francisco was absorbed by God the most Holy Trinity, perceived in the light from Our Lady's hands. After the July apparition, he said, "we were on fire in that light which is God and yet we were not burnt. What is God? ...we could never put it into words". Jacinta said: "I love Our Lord so much. At times I seem to have a fire in my heart, but it does not burn me".

## The Rosary and the Immaculate Heart

Never before in the history of the Church has a revelation of such extraordinary spiritual richness been made through very young children.

As we have seen, Our Lady urged the seers to pray the Rosary every day, and in her final apparition she revealed, "I am the Lady of the Rosary".

In the apparition of 13th June, Lucia asked Our Lady to take the enraptured seers to heaven.

Yes. I will take Jacinta and Francisco soon. But you are to stay here some time longer. Jesus wishes to make use of you to make me known and loved. He wants to establish in the world devotion to my Immaculate Heart. I promise salvation to those who embrace it, and those souls will be loved by God like flowers placed by me to adorn his throne.

Francisco and Jacinta died aged almost eleven and almost ten on 4th April 1919 and 20th February 1920 respectively, having faithfully borne witness to Our Lady's message through their lives of heroic virtue. Lucia died aged almost ninety eight on 13th February 2005, after fulfilling her mission, in the letters she wrote to the popes and many people, and through her books.

"Am I to stay here alone?" Lucia asked sadly. "No," replied Our Lady. "Don't lose heart. I will never forsake you. My Immaculate Heart will be your refuge and the way that will lead you to God" (*FILOW*, p. 177). These last touching words expressing Mary's maternal consolation form a simple yet deeply meaningful prayer.

The words of Jesus on the cross, "behold your son... behold your mother" (*Jn* 19:26, 27) show that devotion to Mary is his will for us, because filial devotion to Mary increases our intimacy with Jesus "and leads to the highest levels of perfection" (Pope St John Paul II, *Theotokos*, p. 192). The reason is that "among creatures no one knows Christ better than Mary, no one can introduce us to a profound knowledge of his mystery better than his Mother" (Pope St John Paul II, *Rosarium Virginis Mariae*, 14). Accordingly, "the Church's devotion to the Blessed Virgin is an intrinsic element of Christian worship" (Pope St Paul VI, *Marialis Cultus*, 56).

### Your Will be Done

With regard to the Immaculate Heart of Mary, Pope Benedict XVI said that it resembles the Heart of Christ more than any other, and earlier as Cardinal Ratzinger he wrote that "to be devoted to the Immaculate Heart of Mary means to embrace this attitude of heart which makes the *fiat* – 'your will be done' – the defining centre of one's whole life" (*Theological Commentary* on the third part of the secret, in *FILOW*, p. 228).

At the end of her second apparition, the children saw the Immaculate Heart of Mary pierced by thorns which encircled it, "outraged by the sins of humanity, and seeking reparation" (*FILOW*, p. 177).

In the apparition of 13th July, in response to Lucia's request, Our Lady promised that in October she would perform a miracle "for all to see and believe". This was the stupendous miracle of the sun, seen by some seventy thousand people from all over Portugal, and which even unbelievers who had come to mock were obliged to affirm. Then she told them to sacrifice themselves for sinners, and to say many times, especially when they did so: "O Jesus, it is for love of you, for the conversion of sinners, and in reparation for the sins committed against the Immaculate Heart of Mary". Using this prayer we can help Jesus to save souls by offering up as a sacrifice anything that happens in daily life that irritates us or upsets our plans.

## A Vision of Hell

Then follows a very realistic description of hell, which they saw in the light from Our Lady's hands. "The Church affirms the existence of hell and its eternity" but only those go there "who to the end of their lives refuse to believe and be converted" (*CCC* 1035, 1034). Pope Francis wants us to take seriously the existence of the devil and his strategies to tempt us into sin, and has said the devil's greatest achievement has been to make us believe he doesn't exist (cf. *Who is the Devil?* p. 3).

As the vision ended, Our Lady explained, so kindly and sadly, the particular reason that the seers were shown hell "where the souls of poor sinners go" because "*to save them* God wishes to establish in the world devotion to my Immaculate Heart" (author's emphasis). Little Jacinta was so touched by the loss and suffering of souls in hell, she said to Lucia: "Why doesn't Our Lady show hell to sinners. If they saw it, they would not sin".

As the vision terminated, Our Lady uttered a grave and prophetic pronouncement which directly concerns the history of the Church and the world in our times.

She warned that if people did not heed her requests to cease offending God, Russia would spread her errors of atheism throughout the world, causing wars and persecutions of the Church, the suffering of the Holy Father and the annihilation of various nations. Is not this happening in our time, in the Middle East and other countries? Russia's errors, inaugurated by Lenin's Communist Revolution in October 1917, the same month of Our Lady's final apparition at Fatima, involved the attempt to install throughout the world political regimes dedicated to the elimination of God and the Church, which resulted in campaigns of immense destruction and the persecution, slaughter and imprisonment of countless millions. In some countries that continues to this day.

In our time the unprecedented world-wide denial and rejection of God has become more prevalent than ever, through the culture of death, the dictatorship of relativism denounced by Benedict XVI, materialism, and the "silent apostasy" in European culture of those who live as if God does not exist (*Ecclesia in Europa*, n. 9).

Our Lady then revealed heaven's response to these grave threats to mankind's salvation, which comprised, at the level of the whole Church, the pope's consecration of Russia to her Immaculate Heart, together with the faithful's Five First Saturdays Communion in reparation to her Immaculate Heart for the blasphemies and ingratitude with which it is pierced by ungrateful men (cf. *Lk* 2:35; *FILOW*, pp. 178, 179, 193-198).

The miraculous outcome of Pope St John Paul II's act of consecration demonstrated that the unfolding of future events depends on our response to Our Lady's requests, and this was endorsed by the verdict of Benedict XVI on his pilgrimage to Fatima in May 2010: "we would be mistaken to think that Fatima's prophetic mission is complete" (*Shepherds of Fatima*, p. 41).

## The Five First Saturdays Devotion

The Five First Saturdays devotion, in reparation to the Immaculate Heart of Mary – the counterpart of the same request that pertains to the faithful – still awaits official approval and implementation by the Church. Little Jacinta was graced with an extraordinary love for Jesus and the Immaculate Heart of Mary. Not long before her death she told Lucia:

> Make known that God wishes to establish in the world devotion to the Immaculate Heart of Mary and that the Heart of Jesus wants the Immaculate Heart of Mary to be venerated at his side. Tell them also to pray to the Immaculate Heart of Mary for peace since God has entrusted it to her. [Pope St John Paul II's act of consecration to the Immaculate Heart of Mary brought the Cold War to an end and peace and reunification for East and West Europe]. If I could only put into the hearts of all the fire that is burning within my own heart, and that makes me love the Hearts of Jesus and Mary so very much. (*FILOW*, p. 132)

## Teaching us to Pray the Rosary

Next, Our Lady conveyed the urgency of Jesus's thirst on the cross to save souls, when she taught the seers to say this prayer after each mystery of the Rosary:

"O my Jesus, forgive us our sins, save us from the fire of hell. Lead all souls to heaven, especially those who are most in need of thy mercy" (*FILOW*, p. 179).

In August Our Lady urged the seers to "pray very much and make sacrifices for sinners, for many souls go to hell (cf. *Mt* 7:13-14) because there are none to sacrifice themselves and to pray for them" (*FILOW*, p. 180). By this simple offering of sacrifices in the ordinary course of daily life we can help Jesus to save souls. Are we following the example of the seers and doing it?

In the final apparition on 13th October 1917, Our Lady said that she wanted a chapel to be built in her honour, and then, "I am the Lady of the Rosary. Continue always to pray the Rosary every day," as she had urged in each of the previous five apparitions.

Finally, looking very sad, Our Lady said: "Do not offend the Lord our God any more, because he is already so much offended."

At this point, while the huge crowd of some seventy thousand people was gazing awestruck at the stupendous miracle of the sun, which appeared to descend to the earth giving out rays of different hues before returning to its place in the sky, the seers saw the Holy Family, with

St Joseph and the Child Jesus blessing the world, then Our Lady of Sorrows, and finally Our Lady of Carmel (*FILOW*, pp. 182, 183).

## The Divine Message of Fatima

The Blessed Virgin's divine message at Fatima issued from her Immaculate Heart – the only heart in the Church which the devil is completely unable to influence with all his insidious strategies for our undoing, and which she promised will triumph "in the end". This is why we need to have recourse to her, in order to overcome the world, the sins of the flesh and the malicious scheming of the devil, by complying with her simple requests. It was their fidelity and commitment in responding to her requests, said Pope St John Paul II, and not the exceptional supernatural manifestations with which they were favoured, which led to Francisco and Jacinta becoming the first child saints in the history of the Church who died, not as martyrs, but in the ordinary course of their family life.

In order to successfully confront the enemy, and advance the New Evangelisation, and ensure the salvation of our souls and those of our families, let us follow their example and entrust ourselves to Our Lady and the message she gave us at Fatima. The lives of Saints Francisco and Jacinta demonstrate that one hundred years later, this message is more relevant than ever.

# Fatima Prayers and Devotions

*compiled by Donal Anthony Foley*

### Morning Offering

O my God, in union with the Immaculate Heart of Mary [*here kiss your brown scapular as a sign of your consecration – this carries a partial indulgence*], I offer you the precious blood of Jesus from all the altars throughout the world, joining with it the offering of my every thought, word and action of this day.

O my Jesus, I desire today to gain every indulgence and merit I can, and I offer them together with myself, to Mary Immaculate, that she may best apply them to the interests of thy most Sacred Heart.

Precious Blood of Jesus, *save us.*

Sorrowful and Immaculate Heart of Mary, *pray for us.*

Sacred Heart of Jesus, *have mercy on us.*

### Pardon Prayer

My God, I believe, I adore, I hope and I love you. I ask pardon of you for those who do not believe, do not adore, do not hope and do not love you.

## Angel's Reparation Prayer

Most Holy Trinity, Father, Son and Holy Spirit, I adore you profoundly and I offer you the most precious body, blood, soul and divinity of Jesus Christ, present in all the tabernacles of the world, in reparation for the outrages, sacrileges and indifference with which he himself is offended. And through the infinite merits of his most Sacred Heart and the Immaculate Heart of Mary, I beg of you the conversion of poor sinners.

## Decade Prayer

O my Jesus, forgive us our sins, save us from the fires of hell. Lead all souls to heaven, especially those most in need of thy mercy.

## Eucharistic Prayer

O most Holy Trinity, I adore you. My God, my God, I love you in the most Blessed Sacrament.

## Sacrifice Prayer

O Jesus, it is for love of you, for the conversion of sinners, and in reparation for the sins committed against the Immaculate Heart of Mary.

## Prayer to Saints Jacinta and Francisco Marto

O God of goodness and font of holiness, who gave Saints Francisco and Jacinta Marto as lights to illuminate the world, exalt the humble who in your light see the light, so that all may contemplate the ways that lead to your heart. Through Our Lord Jesus Christ, your Son, who lives and reigns with you in the unity of the Holy Spirit, one God for ever and ever. Amen.

Our Father, Hail Mary, Glory be...

Please send details of any favours received through the intercession of Saints Francisco and Jacinta, to: Fundacao de Francisco e Jacinta Marto, Rua de Sao Pedro, n. 9, Apartado 6, 2496-908 Fatima – Portugal. Email: secretariado@pastorinhos.com

## Prayer for the Beatification of the Servant of God Sr Lucia

Most Holy Trinity, Father, Son and Holy Spirit, I adore you profoundly and I thank you for the apparitions of the Blessed Virgin Mary in Fatima that revealed to the world the riches of her Immaculate Heart. By the infinite merits of the Sacred Heart of Jesus and through the intercession of the Immaculate Heart of Mary, I implore you, if it should be for your greater glory and the good of our souls, to glorify Sr Lucia, one of the Shepherds of Fatima, by granting us the grace which we implore through her intercession. Amen.

Our Father, Hail Mary, Glory be...

Please send details of any favours received though Sr Lucia's intercession to: Carmelo de Santa Teresa, Rua de Santa Teresa, no 16, 3000-359, Coimbra, Portugal. causabeatificacaolucia@lucia.pt

# Our Lady of Fatima
# and the Rosary

At every one of her six Fatima apparitions between May and October 1917, Our Lady specifically asked for the Rosary to be said. This aspect of her message could not have been more emphatic.

On 13th May 1917, she said: "Pray the Rosary every day to obtain peace for the world and an end to the war."

On 13th June: "I want you to pray the Rosary every day."

On 13th July: "I want you to continue to pray the Rosary every day in honour of Our Lady of the Rosary, to obtain peace for the world and the end of the war because only she can help you."

On 19th August: "Continue praying the Rosary every day."

On 13th September: "Continue to pray the Rosary every day in order to obtain the end of the war."

And on 13th October: "I am the Lady of the Rosary. Continue always to pray the Rosary every day."

**Rosary Meditations Based on the New Testament
and the Fatima Message**

## The Joyful Mysteries
### The Annunciation

In the sixth month the angel Gabriel was sent by God to a town in Galilee called Nazareth, to a virgin betrothed to a man named Joseph, of the House of David; and the virgin's name was Mary. He went in and said to her, "Rejoice, so highly favoured, the Lord is with you." (*Lk* 1:26-28)

I have come to ask you to come here for six months in succession, on the 13th day, at this same hour. Later on, I will tell you who I am and what I want. Afterwards, I will return here yet a seventh time.

(Our Lady to the children, 13th May 1917, *FILOW*, p. 175)

### The Visitation

Mary set out at that time and went as quickly as she could to a town in the hill country of Judaea. She went into Zechariah's house and greeted Elizabeth. Now as soon as Elizabeth heard Mary's greeting, the child leapt in her womb and Elizabeth was filled with the Holy Spirit. (*Lk* 1:39-41)

This meeting of Our Lady and her cousin St Elizabeth shows us Mary's great faith and deep humility... And thinking always of God's mercy, Mary answers her cousin: "My soul magnifies the Lord and my spirit rejoices in

God my Saviour, for he has regarded the low estate of his handmaiden" (*Lk* 1:46-48). The Virgin Mary and St Elizabeth intone here the most beautiful canticle of praise to God. Their lips are moved by the Holy Spirit. But, after all, was not Mary the living temple of the adorable Trinity?

(*Calls from the Message of Fatima* by Sr Lucia, p. 275; p. 276)

### The Nativity

So Joseph set out from the town of Nazareth in Galilee and travelled up to Judaea, to the town of David called Bethlehem, since he was of David's House and line, in order to be registered together with Mary, his betrothed, who was with child. (*Lk* 2:4-5)

In the third decade of the Rosary, we recall the birth of Jesus Christ, God made man. He is the masterpiece of love, God who comes down from heaven to earth to save his poor creatures… He came into the world as a man and manifested himself as Light, Light which shines in the darkness: present among us today as then, but his humanity is veiled. He is present in his word and in his works, in the Eucharist and in the sacraments of the Church and in the person of each of our brothers and sisters.

(*Calls from the Message of Fatima*, p. 276)

### The Presentation in the Temple

And when the day came for them to be purified as laid down by the Law of Moses, they took him up to Jerusalem to present him to the Lord. (*Lk* 2:22)

"O Lord, make me a saint. Keep my heart always pure, for you alone." Then it seemed that in the depths of my heart, our dear Lord distinctly spoke these words to me: "The grace granted to you this day will remain living in your soul, producing fruits of eternal life."

(On the occasion of Lucia's first Holy Communion, *FILOW*, p. 73)

*The Finding of the Child Jesus in the Temple*

Every year his parents used to go to Jerusalem for the feast of the Passover. When he was twelve years old, they went up for the feast as usual. When they were on their way home after the feast, the boy Jesus stayed behind in Jerusalem without his parents knowing it... They were overcome when they saw him, and his mother said to him, "My child, why have you done this to us? See how worried your father and I have been, looking for you." "Why were you looking for me?" he replied. "Did you not know that I must be busy with my Father's affairs?" (*Lk* 2:41-42; 48-49)

"Are you willing to offer yourselves to God to bear all the sufferings he wills to send you, as an act of reparation for the sins by which he is offended, and of supplication for the conversion of sinners?"

"Yes, we are willing," was our reply.

"Then, you are going to have much to suffer, but the grace of God will be your comfort."

(Our Lady to the children, 13th May 1917, *FILOW*, p. 175)

## The Mysteries of Light

### *The Baptism in the Jordan*

As soon as Jesus was baptised he came up from the water, and suddenly the heavens opened and he saw the Spirit of God descending like a dove and coming down on him. And a voice spoke from heaven, "This is my Son, the Beloved; my favour rests on him." (*Mt* 3:16-17)

Suddenly the whole chapel was illumined by a supernatural light, and above the altar appeared a cross of light, reaching to the ceiling. In a brighter light on the upper part of the cross, could be seen the face of a man and his body as far as the waist, upon his breast was a dove also of light and nailed to the cross was the body of another man.

(Sr Lucia's vision of the Trinity, 13th June 1929, *FILOW*, p. 197)

### *The Wedding at Cana*

The mother of Jesus said to him, "They have no wine." Jesus said, "Woman, why turn to me? My hour has not come yet." His mother said to the servants, "Do whatever he tells you." (*Jn* 2:3-5)

You have seen hell where the souls of poor sinners go. To save them, God wishes to establish in the world devotion to my Immaculate Heart. If what I say to you is done, many souls will be saved and there will be peace.

(Our Lady to the children, 13th July 1917, *FILOW*, p. 210)

### The Proclamation of the Kingdom of God

After John had been arrested, Jesus went into Galilee. There he proclaimed the Good News from God. "The time has come," he said "and the kingdom of God is close at hand. Repent, and believe the Good News." (*Mk* 1:14-15)

The insistent invitation of Mary most Holy to penance is nothing but the manifestation of her maternal concern for the fate of the human family, in need of conversion and forgiveness.

(Pope St John Paul II, Message for the 1997 World Day of the Sick)

### The Transfiguration

He took with him Peter and John and James and went up the mountain to pray. As he prayed, the aspect of his face was changed and his clothing became brilliant as lightning (*Lk* 9:28-29)

We beheld a Lady all dressed in white. She was more brilliant than the sun, and radiated a light more clear and intense than a crystal glass filled with sparkling water, when the rays of the burning sun shine through it.

(Sr Lucia describing Our Lady's appearance on 13th May 1917, *FILOW*, p. 174)

### The Institution of the Eucharist

When evening came he was at table with the twelve disciples. Now as they were eating, Jesus took some bread, and when he had said the blessing he broke it and gave it to the disciples. "Take it and eat;" he said "this is my body." Then he took a cup, and when he had returned thanks he gave it to them. "Drink all of you from this," he said "for this is my blood, the blood of the covenant, which is to be poured out for many for the forgiveness of sins." (*Mt* 26:20; 26-28)

I brought Jacinta a picture of a chalice with a host. She took it, kissed it, and radiant with joy she exclaimed: "It is the hidden Jesus, I love him so much. If only I could receive him in church. Don't they receive Holy Communion in heaven? If they do, then I will go to Holy Communion every day."

(Jacinta, while ill, speaking to Lucia, *FILOW*, p. 133)

### The Sorrowful Mysteries

*The Agony in the Garden*

They came to a small estate called Gethsemane, and Jesus said to his disciples, "Stay here while I pray." Then he took Peter and James and John with him. And a sudden fear came over him, and great distress. And he said to them, "My soul is sorrowful to the point of death. Wait here, and keep awake." (*Mk* 14:32-35)

Here as in the other events of his life, Jesus Christ is for us a model, which we must follow and seek to imitate. Although he was God and had, therefore, all grace and strength, he was also truly human; and he chose to prepare himself by prayer, to submit his human will to that of the Father, who needed him as an expiatory victim for the sins of humanity. (*Calls from the Message of Fatima*, p. 281)

### The Scourging at the Pillar

Then he released Barabbas for them. He ordered Jesus to be first scourged and then handed over to be crucified. (*Mt* 27:26)

I've such pains in my chest, but I don't say anything. I'm suffering for the conversion of sinners… I'll suffer for love of Our Lord, to make reparation to the Immaculate Heart of Mary, for the conversion of sinners and for the Holy Father. (Jacinta to Lucia, *FILOW*, p. 59; p. 60)

### The Crowning with Thorns

Then they stripped him and made him wear a scarlet cloak, and having twisted some thorns into a crown they put this on his head and placed a reed in his right hand. To make fun of him they knelt to him saying, "Hail, king of the Jews." (*Mt* 27:28-29)

The evening before she fell sick, Jacinta said: "I've a terrible headache and I'm so thirsty. But I won't take a drink, because I want to suffer for sinners."

On another occasion I noticed, as we left the house, that Francisco was walking very slowly:

"What's the matter?" I asked him. "You seem unable to walk!"

"I've such a bad headache, and I feel as though I'm going to fall."

"Then don't come. Stay at home."

"l don't want to. I'd rather stay in the church with the hidden Jesus".

(*FILOW*, p. 161)

### *The Carrying of the Cross*

They then took charge of Jesus, and carrying his own cross he went out of the city to the place of the skull or, as it was called in Hebrew, Golgotha. (*Jn* 19:17)

Sacrifice yourselves for sinners, and say many times, especially when you make some sacrifice: O Jesus, it is for love of you, for the conversion of sinners, and in reparation for the sins committed against the Immaculate Heart of Mary.

(Our Lady to the children, 13th July 1917, *FILOW*, p. 179)

### *The Crucifixion and Death of Our Lord*

When they reached the place called The Skull, they crucified him there and the two criminals also, one on the right, the other on the left. Jesus said, "Father, forgive them; they do not know what they are doing." (*Lk* 23:33-34)

"You at least try to console me and say that I promise to assist at the hour of death, with the graces necessary for salvation, all those who, on the first Saturday of five consecutive months, shall confess, receive Holy

Communion, recite five decades of the Rosary, and keep me company for fifteen minutes while meditating on the fifteen mysteries of the Rosary, with the intention of making reparation to me."

(Our Lady to Sr Lucia, 10th December 1925, *FILOW*, p. 194)

## The Glorious Mysteries

### *The Resurrection*

The angel spoke; and he said to the women, "There is no need for you to be afraid. I know you are looking for Jesus, who was crucified. He is not here, for he has risen, as he said he would. Come and see the place where he lay, then go quickly and tell his disciples." (*Mt* 28:5-7)

I will take Jacinta and Francisco [to heaven] shortly; but you will stay here for some time to come. Jesus wants to use you to make me known and loved. He wishes to establish the devotion to my Immaculate Heart throughout the world. I promise salvation to whoever embraces it; these souls will be dear to God, like flowers put by me to adorn his throne.

(Our Lady to the children, 13th June 1917, *FILOW*, p. 194)

### *The Ascension of Christ into Heaven*

He was lifted up while they looked on, and a cloud took him from their sight. (*Ac* 1:9)

Then Our Lady began to rise serenely, going up towards the east, until she disappeared in the immensity of space.

The light that surrounded her seemed to open up a path before her in the firmament.

(Our Lady's return to heaven, 13th May 1917, *FILOW*, p. 176)

### The Descent of the Holy Spirit

When Pentecost day came round, they had all met in one room, when suddenly they heard what sounded like a powerful wind from heaven, the noise of which filled the entire house in which they were sitting; and something appeared to them that seemed like tongues of fire; these separated and came to rest on the head of each of them. (*Ac* 2:1-4)

One day during Jacinta's illness, she told Lucia: "I so like to tell Jesus that I love him. Many times, when I say it to him, I seem to have a fire in my heart, but it doesn't burn me." Another time she said: "I love Our Lord and Our Lady so much, that I never get tired of telling them that I love them."

(Jacinta speaking to Lucia, *FILOW*, p. 56)

### The Assumption

Those who have died in Christ will be the first to rise, and then those of us who are still alive will be taken up in the clouds, together with them; to meet the Lord in the air. So we shall stay with the Lord for ever. With such thoughts as these you should comfort one another. (1 *Th* 4:17-18)

One day Lucia asked Jacinta: "What are you going to do in heaven?" She replied: "I'm going to love Jesus very much,

and the Immaculate Heart of Mary, too. I'm going to pray a lot for you, for sinners, for the Holy Father, for my parents and my brothers and sisters, and for all the people who have asked me to pray for them".
(*FILOW*, p. 62)

### The Coronation of Our Lady in Heaven and the Glory of the Saints

Now a great sign appeared in heaven: a woman, adorned with the sun, standing on the moon, and with the twelve stars on her head for a crown. (*Rv* 12:1)

When you pray the Rosary, say after each mystery: "O my Jesus, forgive us, save us from the fire of hell. Lead all souls to heaven, especially those who are most in need." (Decade Prayer, *FILOW*, p. 179)

I am the Lady of the Rosary. Continue always to pray the Rosary every day... Do not offend the Lord our God any more, because he is already so much offended.
(Our Lady's last words, 13th October 1917, *FILOW*, p. 182)

# ACTS OF CONSECRATION
# AND REPARATION

**Consecration to the Immaculate Heart of Mary**

Virgin Mary, Mother of God and our Mother, to your Immaculate Heart we consecrate ourselves, in an act of total entrustment to the Lord. By you we will be led to Christ. By him and with him we will be led to the Father. We will walk in the light of faith, and we will do everything so that the world may believe that Jesus Christ is the one sent by the Father. With him we wish to carry his love and salvation to the ends of the earth. Under the protection of your Immaculate Heart, we will be one people with Christ. We will be witnesses of his Resurrection. By him we will be led to the Father, for the glory of the most Holy Trinity, whom we adore, praise and bless for ever. Amen.

## A Solemn Act of Consecration to the Immaculate Heart of Mary by Pope Pius XII

Most Holy Virgin Mary, tender Mother of men, to fulfil the desires of the Sacred Heart of Jesus and the request of the Vicar of your Son on earth, we consecrate ourselves and our families to your Sorrowful and Immaculate Heart,

O Queen of the most Holy Rosary, and we recommend to you all the people of our country and all the world.

Please accept our consecration, dearest Mother, and use us as you wish to accomplish your designs in the world.

O Sorrowful and Immaculate Heart of Mary, Queen of the most Holy Rosary, and Queen of the World, rule over us, together with the Sacred Heart of Jesus Christ, our King.

Save us from the spreading flood of modern paganism; kindle in our hearts and homes the love of purity, the practice of a virtuous life, an ardent zeal for souls, and a desire to pray the Rosary more faithfully.

We come with confidence to you, O Throne of Grace and Mother of Fair Love. Inflame us with the same divine fire which has inflamed your own Sorrowful and Immaculate Heart. Make our hearts and homes your shrine, and through us make the Heart of Jesus, together with your rule, triumph in every heart and home. Amen.

(Venerable Pope Pius XII as at: *www.ewtn.com/catholicism/devotions/ solemn-act-of-consecration-to-the-immaculate-heart-of-mary-12729*)

### Act of Reparation to the Immaculate Heart of Mary

Holy Virgin Mary, our dear Mother, in showing us your Heart encircled with thorns, symbols of the blasphemies and ingratitude with which men, ungrateful men, repay the tenderness of your love, you asked us to console you and make reparation.

Therefore we humbly approach to make reparation to your Immaculate Heart, and in a special way to atone for the indignities directed towards your Immaculate Conception and holy virginity.

There are many who deny that you are the Mother of God, and will not accept you as the tender Mother of men. Others pour out upon your sacred images their uncontrolled hate, or seek to instil in men's hearts, especially in the hearts of innocent children, indifference and contempt towards you.

Most Holy Virgin, we wish to show the sorrow we feel because of these offences, and we promise to make reparation with our sacrifices, Holy Communions and prayers for the sins of your ungrateful children. Recognising that we ourselves do not always honour and love you as we should, we humbly ask your merciful forgiveness.

# OTHER MARIAN PRAYERS

### The Angelus

V. The angel of the Lord declared unto Mary,
R. *And she conceived of the Holy Spirit.*
Hail Mary…
V. Behold the handmaid of the Lord.
R. *Be it done to me according to thy word.*
Hail Mary…
V. And the word was made flesh,
R. *And dwelt among us.*
Hail Mary…
V. Pray for us O holy Mother of God,
R. *That we may be made worthy of the promises of Christ.*

Let us pray:
Pour forth, we beseech thee O Lord, thy grace into our hearts that we to whom the incarnation of Christ, thy Son, was made known by the message of an angel, may by his Passion and Cross be brought to the glory of his Resurrection: through the same Christ, Our Lord.
R. *Amen.*

## The Regina Caeli – Queen of Heaven

V. O Queen of Heaven, rejoice, alleluia.
R. *For he whom you did merit to bear, alleluia.*
V. Has risen, as he said, alleluia.
R. *Pray for us to God, alleluia.*
V. Rejoice and be glad, O Virgin Mary, alleluia.
R. *For the Lord has truly risen, alleluia.*

Let us pray:
O God, who gave joy to the world through the Resurrection of thy Son, Our Lord Jesus Christ, grant, we beseech thee, that through the intercession of the Virgin Mary, his Mother, we may obtain the joys of everlasting life: through the same Christ Our Lord.
R. *Amen.*

## Magnificat

My soul glorifies the Lord, my spirit rejoices in God my saviour. He looks on his servant in her lowliness; henceforth all generations will call me blessed. The Almighty works marvels for me, holy his name. His mercy is from age to age, on those who fear him. He puts forth his arm in strength and scatters the proud hearted. He casts the mighty from their thrones and raises the lowly. He fills the starving with good things, sends the rich away empty. He protects Israel, his servant, remembering his mercy, the mercy promised to our fathers, to Abraham and his sons for ever. Amen.

## Memorare

Remember, O most gracious Virgin Mary, that never was it known that anyone who fled to thy protection, implored thy help, or sought thine intercession was left unaided.

Inspired by this confidence, I fly unto thee, O Virgin of virgins, my Mother; to thee do I come, before thee I stand, sinful and sorrowful. O Mother of the Word Incarnate, despise not my petitions, but in thy mercy hear and answer me. Amen.

## Prayer of St John Bosco to Mary, Help of Christians

Most Holy Virgin Mary, Help of Christians,
how sweet it is to come to your feet
imploring your perpetual help.
If earthly mothers cease not to remember their children,
how can you, the most loving of all mothers forget me?
Grant then to me, I implore you,
your perpetual help in all my necessities,
in every sorrow, and especially in all my temptations.
I ask for your unceasing help for all who are now suffering.
Help the weak, cure the sick, convert sinners.
Grant through your intercessions many vocations
    to the religious life.
Obtain for us, O Mary, Help of Christians,
that having invoked you on earth we may love and
    eternally thank you in heaven. Amen.

# Novenas to
# Our Lady of Fatima

**Short Nine Day Novena to Our Lady of Fatima**

Most Holy Virgin, who has deigned to come to Fatima to reveal to the three little shepherds the treasures of graces hidden in the recitation of the Rosary, inspire our hearts with a sincere love of this devotion, so that by meditating on the mysteries of our redemption that are recalled in it, we may gather the fruits and obtain the conversion of sinners, the conversion of Russia, and this favour that I so earnestly seek...which I ask of you in this novena, for the greater glory of God, for your own honour, and for the good of all people. Amen.

Our Father, Hail Mary, Glory be...

**Longer Nine Day Novena to Our Lady of Fatima**

*Day 1*

Our Lady of the Rosary, the Holy Trinity sent the Angel of Peace to the three shepherd children, Jacinta, Lucia and Francisco, to prepare them for their meetings with you. Take away our fears and by your intercession give us the grace to believe, hope, adore and love God, and also to ask pardon of those who do not believe, nor adore, nor hope, nor love him. May we pray thus, confident that your Immaculate Heart, and the Sacred Heart of Jesus, your Son, are always ready to listen to our prayers.

*Now make your petition to Our Lady of Fatima*
Our Father, Hail Mary, Glory be…

### Day 2

Our Lady of the Rosary, just as the Angel of Peace urged the children to pray fervently because your Immaculate Heart, and the Sacred Heart of Jesus, had merciful designs on them, so also may we have the grace through your intercession to offer our prayers and sacrifices to God, the most High, so that everything we do may become an act of reparation for the sins by which he is offended, and in supplication for sinners. By doing this, particularly through praying the Rosary, may we help to bring peace to the world, while bearing and accepting with patience the sufferings of life.

*Now make your petition to Our Lady of Fatima*
Our Father, Hail Mary, Glory be…

### Day 3

Our Lady of the Rosary, just as the Angel of Peace knelt down before the precious body and blood of your divine Son, and prayed a profound prayer of adoration and reparation for all the sins of mankind, may we too offer prayers of adoration and reparation to God, and partake worthily of Holy Communion; and through the infinite merits of his most Sacred Heart, and your Immaculate Heart, may we earnestly pray for the conversion of sinners.

*Now make your petition to Our Lady of Fatima*

Our Father, Hail Mary, Glory be…

### Day 4

Our Lady of the Rosary, you came from heaven in May 1917 with a message of prayer and peace. You asked the children if they would be willing to offer themselves to God and bear all the sufferings he sent them, as an act of reparation for the conversion of sinners. May we too make such an offering, and accept that, like the children, this may well involve us in suffering, but that the grace of God will also be our comfort.

*Now make your petition to Our Lady of Fatima*

Our Father, Hail Mary, Glory be…

### Day 5

Our Lady of the Rosary, you came from heaven in June 1917 to ask the children to pray the Rosary every day to bring peace to the world. You also asked that devotion to your Immaculate Heart be spread throughout the world, and promised salvation to all who embrace this devotion. Through your intercession may we, too, have the grace to pray the Rosary every day and to embrace this devotion to you, confident that whatever we have to suffer in life, you will never forsake us, in the knowledge that your Immaculate Heart will be our refuge and the way that will lead us to God.

*Now make your petition to Our Lady of Fatima*
Our Father, Hail Mary, Glory be…

### Day 6

Our Lady of the Rosary, you came from heaven in July 1917 to ask the children to continue to pray the Rosary every day to bring peace to the world. You also asked them to sacrifice themselves for sinners, and say many times, especially when they made some sacrifice: "O Jesus, it is for love of you, for the conversion of sinners, and in reparation for the sins committed against the Immaculate Heart of Mary." May we too have the grace to make such sacrifices, both for ourselves and for those in danger of going to hell.

*Now make your petition to Our Lady of Fatima*
Our Father, Hail Mary, Glory be…

### Day 7

Our Lady of the Rosary, you came from heaven in August 1917, and urged the children to continue to say the Rosary every day, and also asked them to "pray, pray very much and make sacrifices for sinners, for many souls go to hell because there are none to sacrifice themselves and to pray for them." May we too have the grace to pray and make sacrifices for ourselves, our families and friends, and the Church and the world.

*Now make your petition to Our Lady of Fatima*
Our Father, Hail Mary, Glory be…

### Day 8

Our Lady of the Rosary, you came from heaven in September 1917 and once more urged the children to pray the Rosary daily. You also told them that God was pleased with their sacrifices. May we, too, have the grace to pray and make sacrifices for the love of God and in reparation for the sins against your Immaculate Heart. You promised the children, too, that you would cure the sick; give us compassion for those who are suffering sickness, and a great faith in your power to heal.

*Now make your petition to Our Lady of Fatima*
Our Father, Hail Mary, Glory be…

### Day 9

Our Lady of the Rosary, you came from heaven in October 1917, asking that a chapel be built in your honour at the Cova da Iria. May we always have the grace to honour you, to pray the Rosary daily, and to pray to you as Our Lady of the Rosary of Fatima. Above all, may we have the grace to take your final words at Fatima to heart: "Do not offend the Lord our God any more, because he is already so much offended."

*Now make your petition to Our Lady of Fatima*
Our Father, Hail Mary, Glory be…

# Fatima and Immaculate Heart Litanies

### Litany of Our Lady of Fatima

Our Lady of Fatima, *pray for our dear country.*

Our Lady of Fatima, *sanctify our clergy.*

Our Lady of Fatima, *make our Catholics more fervent.*

Our Lady of Fatima, *guide and inspire those who govern us.*

Our Lady of Fatima, *cure the sick who confide in thee.*

Our Lady of Fatima, *console the sorrowful who trust in thee.*

Our Lady of Fatima, *help those who invoke thine aid.*

Our Lady of Fatima, *deliver us from all dangers.*

Our Lady of Fatima, *help us to resist temptation.*

Our Lady of Fatima, *obtain for us all that we lovingly ask of thee.*

Our Lady of Fatima, *help those who are dear to us.*

Our Lady of Fatima, *bring back to the right road our erring brothers.*

Our Lady of Fatima, *give us back our ancient fervour.*

Our Lady of Fatima, *obtain for us pardon of our manifold sins and offences.*

Our Lady of Fatima, *bring all men to the feet of thy divine Child.*

Our Lady of Fatima, *obtain peace for the world.*

O Mary conceived without sin, *pray for us who have recourse to thee.*

Immaculate Heart of Mary, *pray for us now and at the hour of our death.* Amen.

Let us pray:

O God of infinite goodness and mercy, fill our hearts with a great confidence in thy dear Mother, whom we invoke under the title of Our Lady of the Rosary and Our Lady of Fatima, and grant us by her powerful intercession all the graces, spiritual and temporal, which we need. Through Christ Our Lord. *Amen.*

Taken from: *https://www.ewtn.com/catholicism/devotions/litany-to-our-lady-of-fatima-254*

## Litany of Blessed Francisco and Jacinta

Lord, have mercy on us, *Lord, have mercy on us.*

Christ, have mercy on us, *Christ, have mercy on us.*

Lord, have mercy on us, *Lord, have mercy on us.*

God the Father, Creator of the world, *have mercy on us.*

God the Son, Redeemer of mankind, *have mercy on us.*

God the Holy Spirit, perfection of those who are chosen, *have mercy on us.*

Holy Trinity, one God, *have mercy on us.*

Holy Mary, Mother of God, *pray for us.*

Our Lady of the Rosary, *pray for us.*

Immaculate Heart of Mary, *pray for us.*

Francisco and Jacinta, children blessed by God, *pray for us.*
Children so dear to the Heart of Our Lady, *pray for us.*
Children so loved by all of us, *pray for us.*

Little shepherds, in admiration of the glories of creation,
   *pray for us.*
Little shepherds, gazing in wonder at the starry sky,
   *pray for us.*
Little shepherds, caressing your furry white lambs,
   *pray for us.*
Little shepherds, with your clear innocent gaze, *pray for us.*
Little shepherds, with your angelic smile, *pray for us.*
Little shepherds, with your pure soul, *pray for us.*

Hearts enchanted by beauty, *pray for us.*
Hearts yearning for truth, *pray for us.*
Hearts overflowing with love, *pray for us.*
Amazing wonders of prayer, *pray for us.*
Wells brimming over with sacrifices, *pray for us.*
Children totally committed and ready for martyrdom,
   *pray for us.*

Francisco, seeker of peace and contemplation, *pray for us.*
You who would console God, *pray for us.*
You who died smiling, *pray for us.*
Jacinta, faithful helpmate of the Holy Father, *pray for us.*
You, the apostle of the Immaculate Heart of Mary,
   *pray for us.*

You, the friend of sinners, *pray for us.*
You two, who enjoyed the company of angels, *pray for us.*
Confidantes of Our Lady, *pray for us.*
Living witnesses of her message, *pray for us.*
You who loved God so deeply, *pray for us.*
Watchers beside the hidden Jesus, *pray for us.*
Adorers of the most Blessed Trinity, *pray for us.*
Stars of light for all human beings, *pray for us.*
Burning bushes of the most High, *pray for us.*
Flames of love for all eternity, *pray for us.*

Lamb of God, who takes away the sins of the world,
   *forgive us, O Lord.*
Lamb of God, who takes away the sins of the world,
   *hear us, O Lord.*
Lamb of God, who takes away the sins of the world,
   *have mercy on us.*

Let us pray:
O God who granted to our two little shepherds the grace to become little burning bushes on fire with love for the Holy Father and for sinners, and burning with love for Our Lady and the "hidden" Jesus, grant that we, too, may be other Franciscos and other Jacintas, so that we, too, may burn with the same love and, with them, all meet together again in heaven around Our Lady in adoration of the Blessed Trinity. Through Jesus Christ. *Amen.*

### Litany of the Immaculate Heart of Mary
### by St John Henry Newman

Lord, have mercy, *Lord, have mercy.*
Christ, have mercy, *Christ, have mercy.*
Lord, have mercy, *Lord, have mercy.*
Christ, hear us, *Christ, graciously hear us.*

God the Father of heaven, *have mercy on us.*
God the Son, Redeemer of the world, *have mercy on us.*
God the Holy Spirit, *have mercy on us.*
Holy Trinity, one God, *have mercy on us.*

Heart of Mary, *pray for us.*
Heart of Mary, after God's own Heart, *pray for us.*
Heart of Mary, in union with the Heart of Jesus, *pray for us.*
Heart of Mary, vessel of the Holy Spirit, *pray for us.*
Heart of Mary, shrine of the Trinity, *pray for us.*
Heart of Mary, home of the Word, *pray for us.*
Heart of Mary, immaculate in your creation, *pray for us.*
Heart of Mary, flooded with grace, *pray for us.*
Heart of Mary, blessed of all hearts, *pray for us.*
Heart of Mary, throne of glory, *pray for us.*
Heart of Mary, abyss of humbleness, *pray for us.*
Heart of Mary, victim of love, *pray for us.*
Heart of Mary, nailed to the cross, *pray for us.*
Heart of Mary, comfort of the sad, *pray for us.*
Heart of Mary, refuge of the sinner, *pray for us.*

Heart of Mary, hope of the dying, *pray for us.*
Heart of Mary, seat of mercy, *pray for us.*

Lamb of God, who takes away the sins of the world,
    *spare us, O Lord.*
Lamb of God, who takes away the sins of the world,
    *graciously hear us, O Lord.*
Lamb of God, who takes away the sins of the world,
    *have mercy on us.*

Christ, hear us, Christ, *graciously hear us.*
Lord, have mercy, *Lord, have mercy.*
Christ, have mercy, *Christ, have mercy.*
Lord, have mercy, *Lord, have mercy.*

V. Immaculate Mary, meek and humble of heart.
R. *Conform our hearts to the Heart of Jesus.*

Let us pray:
O most merciful God, who for the salvation of sinners
and the refuge of the wretched, has made the Immaculate
Heart of Mary most like in tenderness and pity to the Heart
of Jesus, grant that we, who now commemorate her most
sweet and loving heart, may by her merits and intercession,
ever live in the fellowship of the Hearts of both Mother and
Son, through the same Christ Our Lord. *Amen.*

# Fatima Hymns

### Fatima Ave

The thirteenth of May
In the Cova da Iria
Appeared, oh so brilliant,
The Virgin Maria.

*Refrain*
Ave, Ave, Ave Maria (2)

The Virgin Maria
Encircled with light,
Our own dearest Mother
And heaven's delight. *R/.*

To three little shepherds
Our Lady appeared.
The light of her grace
To her Son souls endeared. *R/.*

With war and its evils
The whole world was seething
And countless of thousands
Were mourning and weeping. *R/.*

To save all poor souls
Who had wandered astray,
With sweet words of comfort
She asked us to pray. *R/.*

By honouring Mary
And loving her Son,
The peace of the world
Will most surely be won. *R/.*

### Our Lady of Fatima

O come to the throne of grace,
O come to the heart most pure,
To Mary our hope of life,
In whom salvation is sure.

*Refrain*
Our Lady of Fatima, hail,
Immaculate Mother of Grace,
Oh pray for us, help us today,
Thou hope of the human race.

Immaculate Heart, we kneel,
To consecrate all to thee,
The present, its pain and joy,
The future, all it may be. *R/.*

The sun at thy royal word,
Spun around like a splendid toy,
The rose-petals showering down,
Proclaimed thee cause of our joy. *R/.*


## O Virgin of the Rosary

O Virgin of the Rosary,
Of Fatima, dear Lady,
O dearest Queen of Heaven,
To save you're ever ready.
O Virgin of the Rosary,
Of Fatima, dear lady,
As now we leave your sanctuary,
Once more we kneel before thee.

*Refrain*
Just one more final prayer
As we leave, oh Mother dear,
May our hearts ever ring,
With the words that we sing:
Oh, Fatima, farewell, Mother dear, farewell,
Oh Fatima, farewell, Mother dear, farewell.

Before we leave, oh Mother,
Oh hear our prayer of sorrow,
And save us from all danger
Today, tonight, tomorrow.

Before we leave, oh Mother,
Have mercy on our sorrow
And ever be our guardian,
Today, tonight, tomorrow. *R/.*

Oh Mother, as we leave you,
The tears to our eyes are springing,
But still our hearts with happiness,
Your love, your praise, are singing.
Oh Mother, as we leave you,
Our eyes with tears are dimming,
But though we weep at parting,
Our souls with love are brimming. *R/.*

# The World Apostolate of Fatima

In 2017, the centenary year of Our Lady's apparitions at Fatima, the World Apostolate of Fatima was privileged to take the National Pilgrim Virgin statue (NPVS) of Our Lady of Fatima, to 19 Cathedrals and 3 national shrines in England and Wales, for Mass celebrated by the bishop, who crowned the statue and consecrated the diocese to the Immaculate Heart of Mary. Afterwards members of the apostolate gave formation in the message. The Visitations began with Mass celebrated by Cardinal Vincent Nichols in Westminster Cathedral, when he renewed the consecration of England and Wales to the Immaculate Heart of Mary. This statue was blessed at Fatima in May 1967 by Pope St. Paul VI and presented to us by the Bishop of Fatima in 1968. When Pope St. John Paul II came to England in 1982, he blessed the NPVS at the Apostolic Nunciature in Wimbledon.

In addition, the Centenary Pilgrim Statue of the Immaculate Heart of Mary (see p. 68) will be available for the northern dioceses of England and Wales. Please contact the custodian, Patrick Cunningham, on **padcunningham@gmail.com**.

If you would like to receive a visitation of the NPVS for the southern dioceses, together with relics of Saints Francisco and Jacinta, please contact the NPVS custodian, Nestor Baniqued, via his email: **stamfordnicky@yahoo.co.uk**.

You will need the consent of your parish priest for the visitation, and Nestor or Patrick will be glad to arrange this with him and help you prepare an appropriate programme, including a PowerPoint presentation on Our Lady's message and its relevance in helping the faithful to live their Catholic life today.

Pope St John Paul II said that Fatima is
"a message of conversion and hope …
which is the true Gospel of Christ".

# Bibliography

All biblical quotations are taken from the *New Revised Standard Version*.

Dominican Nuns of Perpetual Rosary (trans.) *Fatima in Lucia's own Words* (16th Edition, no publisher given, July 2007).

Sisters of Mosteiro de Santa Maria and Convento de NS do Bom Success, Lisbon (trans.) *"Calls" from the Message of Fatima* (Secretariado dos Pastorinhos, Fatima, Portugal, 2001) *https://archive.org/details/callsfrommessage00*.

Rev. Nick Donnelly, *Who is the Devil? What Pope Francis Says* (London, Catholic Truth Society, 2014).

Pope Benedict XVI, *Shepherds of Fatima, Pope Benedict XVI's Homilies and Addresses in Portugal* (London, Catholic Truth Society, 2010).

Timothy Tindal-Robertson, *Message of Fatima,* (London, Catholic Truth Society, 1998).

# Images

Page 7: *Lúcia Santos, Jacinta and Francisco Marto*, 1917, photo by Joshua Benoliel © Shrine of Fatima. Page 8: *Sister Maria Lúcia of Jesus and of the Immaculate Heart* © Shrine of Fatima. Page 25: *Our Lady of the Rosary of Fatima* © Shrine of Fatima. Page 47: *Our Lady of the Rosary of Fatima* © Shrine of Fatima. Page 68: *Immaculate Heart of Mary* © Oliver Abasolo.